POCKET FLYERS

PAPER AIRPLANE BOOK

KEN BLACKBURN
& JEFF LAMMERS

WORKMAN PUBLISHING • NEW YORK

To my wife, Karen, for all her support and love. —JL
To all the paper airplane pilots young and old who keep the spirit of flight alive. —KB

Library of Congress Cataloging-in-Publication Data
Blackburn, Ken.
Pocket flyers paper airplane book/Ken Blackburn & Jeff Lammers.
p.   cm.
ISBN 0-7611-1362-2 (pbk.)
1. Paper airplanes—Juvenile literature. 2. Toy and movable books—Specimens. I. Lammers, Jeff. II. Title.
TL778.b58 1998   98-36689 CIP
745.592—dc21

Cover design by Nancy Loggins Gonzalez
Interior design by Nancy Loggins Gonzalez with Erica Heitman
Cover and interior photographs by Walt Chrynwski
Plane graphics: Dragonfly, B-2 Buzz Bomber, Mummy, and Talon by Shi Chen; Saber by Dan Cosgrove;
Rotors by Brad Hamann; Gargoyle by Erica Heitman; Skyhawk by Daniel Pelavin;
U147 Circuit Cruiser, Phoenix, Wizard, and Concorde 500 by Mark Reidy.

Workman books are available at special discount when purchased in bulk for special
premiums and sales promotions as well as for fund-raising or educational use.
Special editions or book excerpts can also be created to specification.
For details, contact the Special Sales Director at the address below.

Workman Publishing Company, Inc.
708 Broadway
New York, NY 10003-9555

Manufactured in the United States of America
First Printing August 1998
10 9 8 7

CONTENTS

WELCOME TO THE WORLD OF MINIATURE AVIATION

In most ways, mini paper airplanes are much like full-size paper planes. They fly for the same reasons and are adjusted the same way, but little planes do have some special characteristics. They are more agile than their bigger counterparts—they turn faster and are more sensitive to adjustments. Their smaller size also gives them the appearance of being very fast (even though they actually fly at the same speed as bigger paper planes).

Mini planes are ideal for indoor flying—in part because there's no wind to buffet them about or to carry them off, and also because they're so tiny, it's easy to lose them outdoors.

BEST-BET FOLDING TIPS

All the pocket flyers are marked with dashed and dotted lines. The dashed lines are what we call "fold-in" lines, which means that they will be on the inside of a crease; you won't be able to see them once you make the fold. They are numbered in the order you should make the folds.

The dotted lines are "fold-away" lines. You'll be able to see them on the outside of the crease; they act as guides to help you know that you're folding in the right place. Some planes require cutting; cut lines are indicated by thick, solid lines.

Try to make your creases as sharp as possible. It's wise to run a fingernail over the edge after you make a fold. This will help especially with the planes that have a lot of folds in one area, like the Saber.

ADJUSTING THE PLANES

Even if you've folded your plane exactly as indicated, there's a good chance that it won't fly well at first. Almost all paper airplanes need a little fine-tuning. Bear in mind that with small paper airplanes, even tiny adjustments can have extreme results. For example, if a little up elevator is required for a

Up
Elevator

level glide, adding only a small amount more may cause the plane to loop.

The first thing to check is that the wings are even and form a "Y" shape with the body.

"Y" SHAPE

UP AND DOWN

Adjusting the elevator is probably the next most important fix—it can keep your plane from stalling (slowing, then swooping to the ground and crashing) or diving. The elevator on a paper airplane is usually located at the back edges of the wings. If your plane is diving, add a little up elevator by bending the back edges

of the wings up a little. If it's stalling, you may have added too much up elevator. Flatten the back edges of the wings.

LEFT AND RIGHT

Most paper airplanes have a tendency to turn when they are first thrown. This can be fixed by adjusting the rudder of the plane. On most paper airplanes, the rudder is the back of the body (or fuselage). To adjust it, bend it a little to the right or left. If your plane isn't flying straight, bend the rudder in the direction you want it to go. For example, if your plane is veering off to the right, bend the rudder a little to the left, and vice versa. If your plane flies straight and you want it to turn right, bend the rudder to the right. Do the opposite for the left.

RUDDER

SENDING THEM SOARING

A good flight requires a good throw. For most planes, your best bet is to pinch the body (fuselage) toward the front, using your thumb and index finger. (The Rotors and the Dragonfly use different throws; they're described in the folding instructions for those planes.)

Hold the plane level just in front of your shoulder and toss it forward.

Each model in this book is unique. Experimentation is the quickest way to learn how a plane flies best. Test-fly your planes, trying different adjustments and faster and slower throws. Generally speaking, the larger and wider the wings, the slower an airplane can successfully fly and the better it will glide. Airplanes with smaller wings usually fly faster and are better suited for long distances. But don't accept our word on this; fold up some planes and find out for yourself!

CONCORDE 500

About 30 years ago, a British and French team developed the Concorde, the fastest passenger plane ever built. It can carry 128 travelers across the Atlantic in less than three hours at more than twice the speed of sound. (It travels about 1,400 miles per hour.) Your Concorde 500 is designed to resemble some of the fastest ground vehicles, Indy racing cars. Use it to set your own air and land records.

✈

FLYING TIPS

It's important to keep this plane's wings symmetrical and in a "Y" shape with the body. With a little up elevator, the Concorde 500 is great for long-distance flights.

MAKING THE CONCORDE 500

FOLD IN ON DASHED LINES (SO THEY ARE NO LONGER VISIBLE); FOLD AWAY ON DOTTED LINES.

1. Fold on lines 1 and 2.

2. Fold on lines 3 and 4.

3. Flip plane over and fold in half on line 5. Cut tail on solid line.

4. Fold one wing down on line 6.

5. Flip plane over and fold other wing on line 7.

6. Open plane and push tail up on line 8. Fold wing tips on lines 9 and 10.

ROTORS

Prepare for an invasion from outer space! Just as flying saucers can land vertically, so can these unique paper aircrafts. Rotors should be launched by throwing them straight up in the air. The blades will stay folded down until the peak of flight, at which point they'll open, and the aircraft will spin down rapidly. Try letting the Rotors fall from a height like the top of a staircase.

FLYING TIPS

It is very important that the blades are bent in a "Y" shape with the body, or this craft will tend to flip upside down and dive.

CUT ON SOLID LINES; FOLD IN ON DASHED LINES
(SO THEY ARE NO LONGER VISIBLE); FOLD AWAY ON DOTTED LINES.

1. Cut Rotors apart along solid lines as shown.

2. Take one Rotor and fold on line 1.

3. Fold on line 2.

4. Fold on lines 3 and 4. Tape closed (optional).

5. Fold blades down on lines 5 and 6.

B-2 BUZZ BOMBER

The shape of this plane was inspired by the B-2 Stealth Bomber and the housefly, even though houseflies are anything but stealthy. They buzz around annoyingly, making their presence well known. Still, they are great flyers—just think about how often they manage to slip out from under the swatter. Like both its namesakes, this plane is an excellent flyer.

✈ FLYING TIPS

Be sure the wings form a slight "Y" shape with the body. A little up elevator on the trailing points will keep this plane from diving.

MAKING THE B-2 BUZZ BOMBER

CUT ON SOLID LINES; FOLD IN ON DASHED LINES
(SO THEY ARE NO LONGER VISIBLE); FOLD AWAY ON DOTTED LINES.

1. Cut as shown.

2. Fold on lines 1 and 2.

3. Fold on line 3.

4. Fold on lines 4 and 5.

5. Flip plane over and fold the plane in half on line 6.

6. Fold one wing down on line 7.

7. Flip plane over and fold the other wing up on line 8.

8. Open up so that wings form a slight "Y" shape with body.

SABER

The saber-toothed tigers that once roamed North America were ferocious, massive creatures with upper canine teeth that could be as long as eight inches. Though this flying tiger is fierce-looking, it's got the heart of a pussycat. It's a high-performance, all-around flyer, good for smooth, long-distance flights.

FLYING TIPS

For normal flight, use a little up elevator and give the plane a gentle toss. To perform loops, add more up elevator and throw the plane straight up.

MAKING THE SABER

FOLD IN ON DASHED LINES (SO THEY ARE NO LONGER
VISIBLE); FOLD AWAY ON DOTTED LINES.

1. Fold on line 1 and reopen. Fold on line 2 and reopen. Flip plane over and fold on line 3 and reopen. Bring points A and B together and fold as shown.

2. Fold on line 4.

4. Fold on line 6, then fold back on line 7.

3. Fold back on line 5.

5. Fold nose down on line 8.

6. Flip plane over and fold in half on line 9.

7. Fold one wing down on line 10.

8. Flip plane over and fold other wing down on line 11.

9. Open plane and fold wing tips up on lines 12 and 13 and fold "teeth" down on lines 14 and 15.

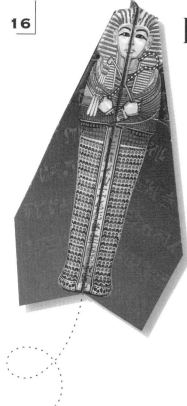

MUMMY

Let this superior glider take you back in time to the pyramids of ancient Egypt and the tomb of an unknown pharaoh. The Mummy is a type of dart plane, but it has more paper in the nose, which gives it extra stability. It's a great long-distance flyer—perfect for trips across the space/time continuum.

FLYING TIPS

The Mummy flies best if you add a little up elevator, but be careful not to add too much because this plane is very sensitive to elevator adjustment.

MAKING THE MUMMY

FOLD IN ON DASHED LINES (SO THEY ARE NO LONGER VISIBLE); FOLD AWAY ON DOTTED LINES.

1. Fold in on lines 1 and 2.

2. Fold up on line 3.

3. Fold on lines 4 and 5.

4. Fold point down on line 6.

5. Flip plane over and fold in half on line 7.

6. Fold one wing down on line 8.

7. Flip plane over and fold other wing down on line 9.

8. Open plane. Make sure the wings form a slight "Y" shape with body.

U147 CIRCUIT CRUISER

Integrated circuits have changed the world. Their miniature size enables them to control everything from a watch to the autopilot system in new jumbo jets, such as the Boeing 777. Your U147 Circuit Cruiser has low-tech mechanicals, but high-tech style. Its wide wings enable it to achieve long, floating flights.

FLYING TIPS

It's important that the wings form a "Y" shape with the body. Add a little up elevator to the points at the back of each wing for best flight.

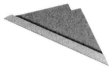

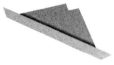

1. Fold on line 1.

2. Fold on line 2.

3. Fold on line 3.

4. Flip plane over and fold on line 4.

5. Fold one wing down on line 5.

6. Flip plane over and fold the other wing down on line 6.

7. Open plane as shown.

8. Fold wing tips up on lines 7 and 8.

TALON

The Talon's wings are broad, just like an owl's. While searching for food, owls glide long distances. Once they have spotted dinner they swoop down silently, snatching up their prey with their mighty talons. When adjusted properly, your Talon will be able to silently glide long distances too. But don't count on it bringing home any rats.

✈ FLYING TIPS

For normal flight, use a little up elevator. Try bending the rudder to the left or right to get your Talon to circle in for the kill!

MAKING THE TALON

CUT ON SOLID LINES; FOLD IN ON DASHED LINES
(SO THEY ARE NO LONGER VISIBLE); FOLD AWAY ON DOTTED LINES.

1. Fold on lines 1 and 2.

2. Fold on line 3.

3. Fold back on line 4.

4. Flip plane over and fold in half on line 5. Cut tail on solid line.

5. Fold one wing down on line 6.

6. Flip plane over and fold other wing down on line 7.

7. Open plane and push tail up on line 8. Fold wing tips up on lines 9 and 10.

SKYHAWK

This Skyhawk resembles one of the most common high-wing aircraft around. It is the Cessna 172, also known as the T-41 Mescalero, 175 Skylark, Cutlass, and Skyhawk. Various versions have been produced since 1956.

The Skyhawk is a very stable, reliable aircraft used by many flight schools to train young aviators. Your Skyhawk should perform just as well.

FLYING TIPS

The Skyhawk requires a paper clip on the nose. Use a little up elevator and a level, gentle toss for this plane. Try putting a little downward bend in the trailing edge of the wings to create more lift for better glides.

MAKING THE SKYHAWK

CUT ON SOLID LINES; FOLD IN ON DASHED LINES
(SO THEY ARE NO LONGER VISIBLE); FOLD AWAY ON DOTTED LINES.

1. Cut apart as shown.

2. Fold wing on line 1.

3. Fold wing on line 2.

4. Fold fuselage in half on line 3.

5. Fold wing tabs down on lines 4 and 5 and horizontal elevators on lines 6 and 7.

6. Tape wing to fuselage where indicated.

7. Tape rudder inside fuselage so that the line on rudder's lower part is flush with top of fuselage. Slip paper clip over nose.

GARGOYLE

Gargoyles usually perch along rooftops their entire lifetime, but your gargoyle is free to go wherever it wants. Use it for any type of flying—indoor or outdoor. The Gargoyle is also an excellent plane for loops and turns. For loops, add a lot of up elevator, then toss the plane straight up. For turns, adjust the rudder to go left or right, then throw it straight ahead.

FLYING TIPS

The Gargoyle may require a few pieces of tape to keep the underside of the wings flat. For best flight, add a small amount of up elevator.

MAKING THE GARGOYLE

CUT ON SOLID LINES; FOLD IN ON DASHED LINES
(SO THEY ARE NO LONGER VISIBLE); FOLD AWAY ON DOTTED LINES.

1. Cut as shown.

2. Fold on lines 1 and 2.

3. Fold on line 3.

4. Fold on lines 4 and 5.

5. Flip plane over and fold on line 6. Cut tail on solid line.

6. Fold one wing down on line 7.

7. Flip plane over and fold other wing down on line 8.

8. Open plane and push tail up on line 9.

DRAGONFLY

A real dragonfly's wide wings and long tail allow it to hover while searching for little insects to eat. Dragonflies appear to be very peaceful, darting prettily over water, but in fact they're active hunters and can consume their own weight in just half an hour. Your dragonfly isn't a big eater, but with a proper throw it will zip about the room. Pinch the back of the tail with your finger and thumb and give it a gentle, level push.

FLYING TIPS

Be sure the wings form a "V" when looking at the plane from the front. Add a little up elevator to the end of the tail to make this plane glide well.

MAKING THE DRAGONFLY

**CUT ON SOLID LINE; FOLD IN ON DASHED LINES
(SO THEY ARE NO LONGER VISIBLE); FOLD AWAY ON DOTTED LINES.**

1. Cut off tail as shown.

2. Fold on line 1 and reopen. Fold on line 2 and reopen. Flip plane over and fold on line 3 and reopen. Bring points A and B together and fold as shown.

3. Flip plane over and fold on line 4.

4. Fold back on line 5.

5. Fold on line 6.

6. Fold back on line 7.

7. Fold nose over on line 8.

8. Fold tabs up on lines 9 and 10.

9. Flip plane over; fold on line 11; reopen. Fold tail on line 12 and partially reopen. Insert tail into body of Dragonfly, as shown.

PHOENIX

The Phoenix is a legendary bird that died
in flames but arose reborn from its ashes.
Your Phoenix is a sleek, graceful flyer.
Remember, if it crashes, try some adjust-
ments and send it soaring again—it's a
Phoenix after all.

✈

FLYING TIPS

For normal flight, use a little up elevator. This plane's
long tail makes it sensitive, so make your adjustments
subtle.

MAKING THE PHOENIX

CUT ON SOLID LINES; FOLD IN ON DASHED LINES
(SO THEY ARE NO LONGER VISIBLE); FOLD AWAY ON DOTTED LINES.

1. Cut as shown. Discard smaller piece.

2. Fold on lines 1 and 2.

3. Fold nose up on line 3.

4. Fold on line 4.

5. Fold nose down on line 5.

6. Flip plane over and fold in half on line 6. Cut tail on solid line.

7. Fold one wing down on line 7.

8. Flip plane over and fold other wing down on line 8.

9. Open up plane and push tail up along line 9.

WIZARD

The wizard works his magic in his cave, but when he ventures out into the world, he takes the form of a raven. Like a raven, this aircraft is a sleek and nimble flyer. If you know the right spells, you can make it do loops and dives (see below).

FLYING TIPS

Since this plane's tail is far from its wings, subtle adjustments will greatly affect each flight. Try extra up elevator and throw straight up for loops. For dives, add up elevator, point the nose down, and drop the plane. It should dive and then swoop up before hitting the floor.

CUT ON SOLID LINES; FOLD IN ON DASHED LINES
(SO THEY ARE NO LONGER VISIBLE); FOLD AWAY ON DOTTED LINES.

1. Cut as shown.

2. Fold on lines 1 and 2.

3. Fold on line 3.

4. Fold nose back on line 4.

5. Fold wings on lines 5 and 6.

6. Flip plane over and fold in half on line 7.

7. Fold one wing down on line 8.

8. Flip plane over and fold other wing down on line 9.

9. Open as shown. Make sure wings form a slight "Y" shape with body of plane.

FLIGHT LOG

KEEP A LOG OF YOUR BEST FLIGHTS—THE LONGEST TIMES ALOFT
AND GREATEST DISTANCES FLOWN

DATE	AIRPLANE NAME	LONGEST TIME ALOFT	GREATEST DISTANCE FLOWN

THE POCKET FLYERS SQUADRON

CONCORDE 500	ROTORS	B-2 BUZZ BOMBER	SABER
MUMMY	U147 CIRCUIT CRUISER	TALON	SKYHAWK
GARGOYLE	DRAGONFLY	PHOENIX	WIZARD

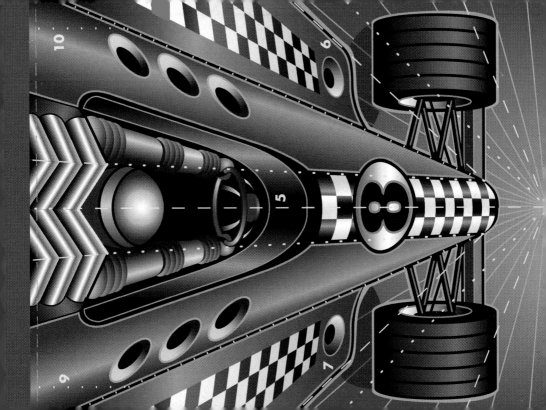

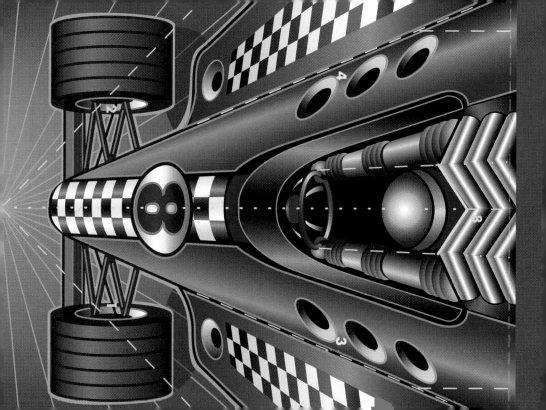

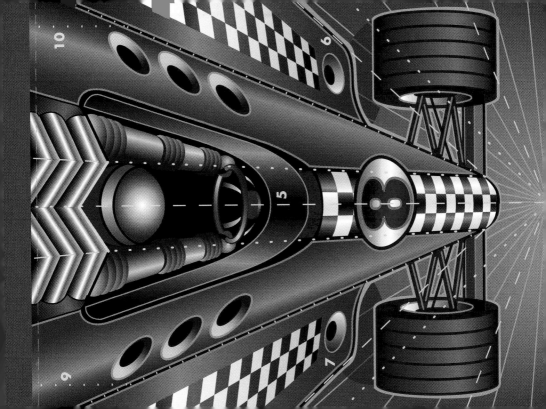

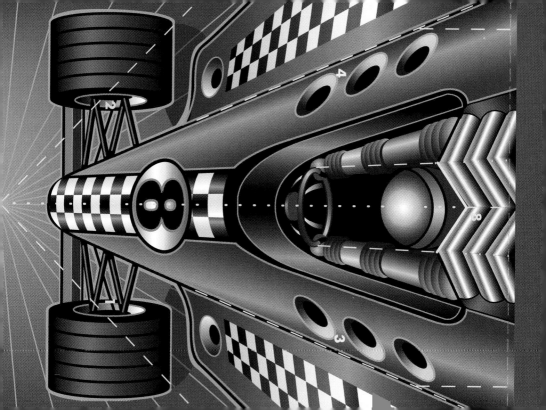

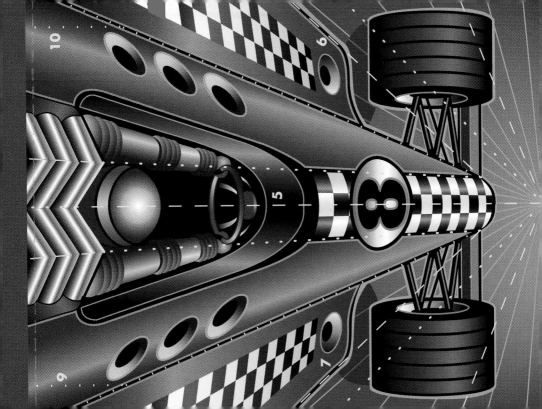

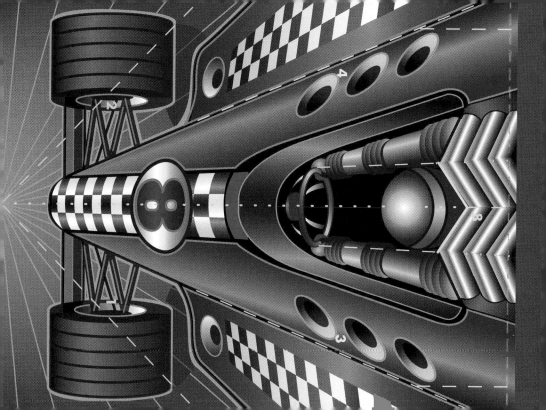

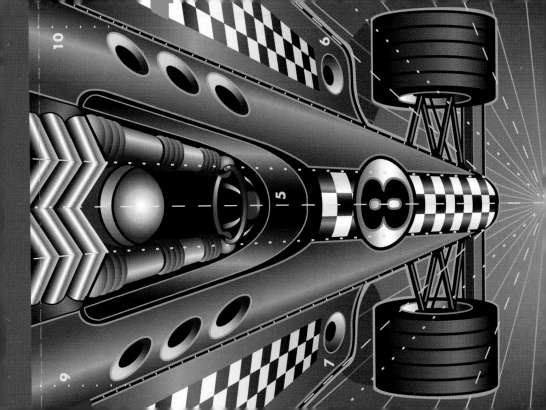

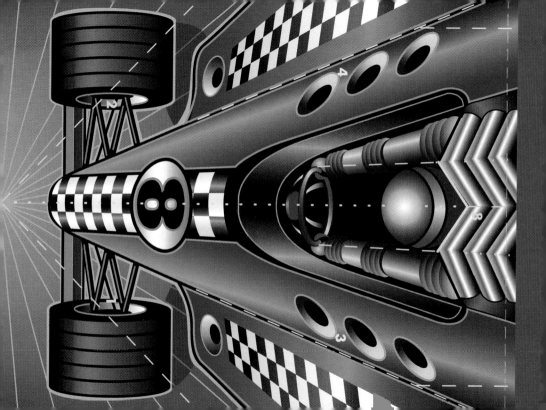

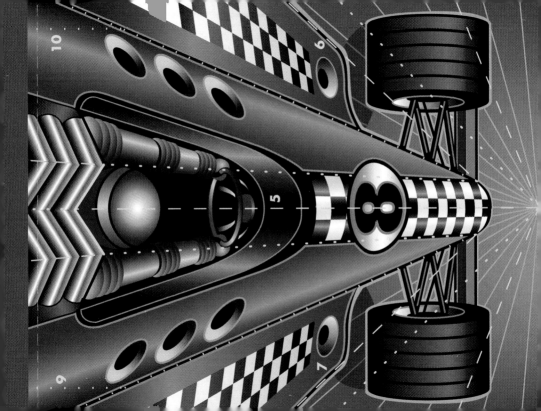

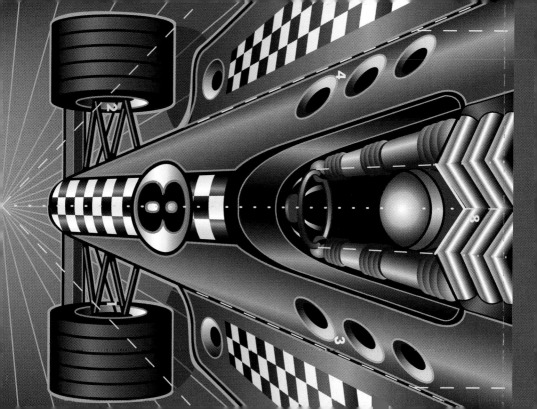

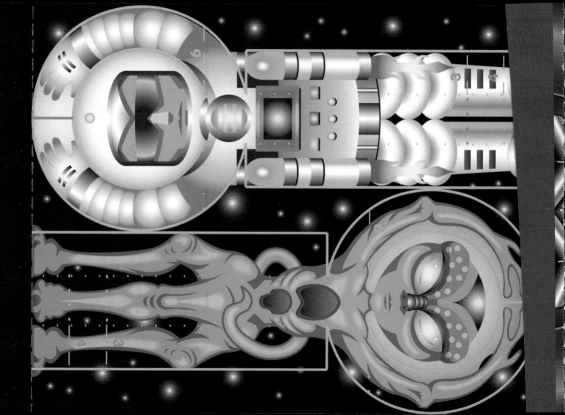

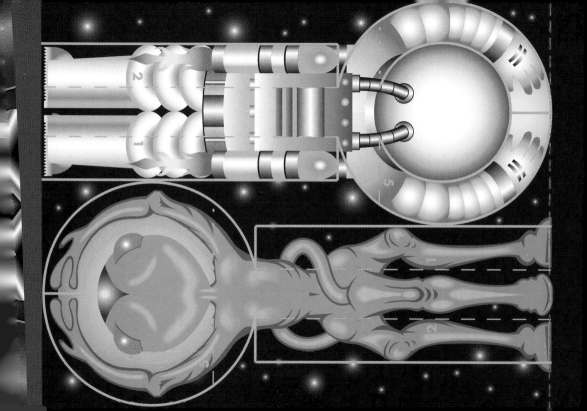

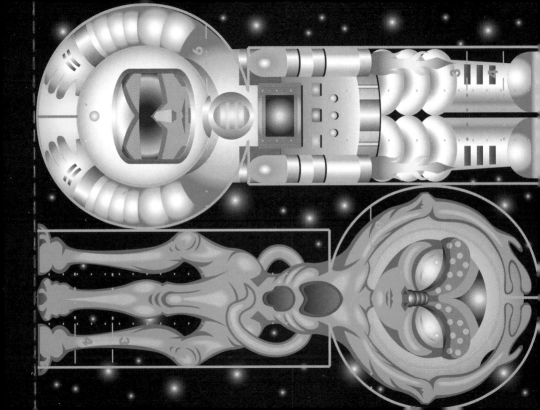

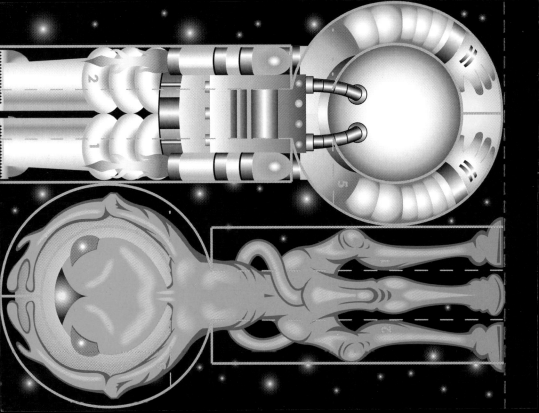

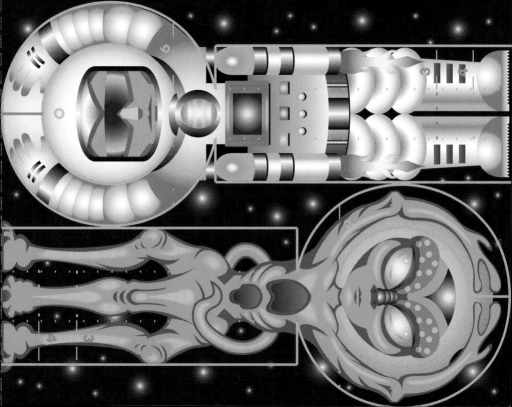

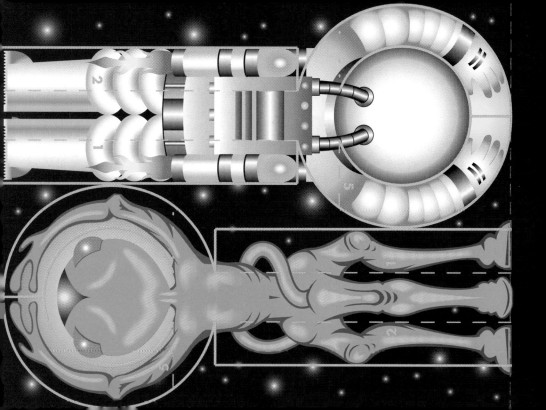

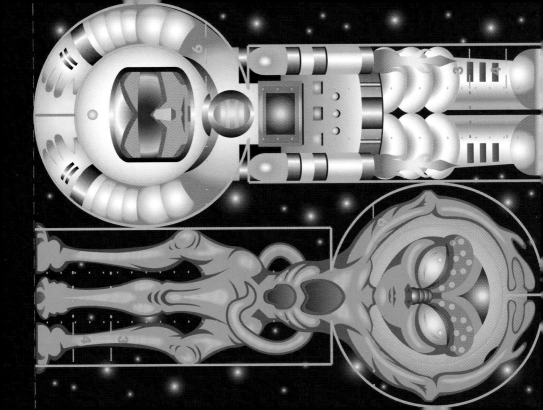

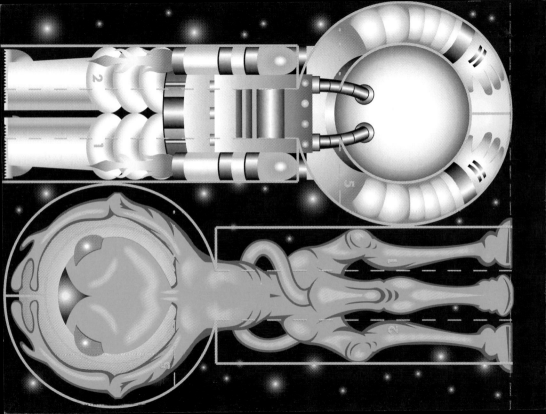

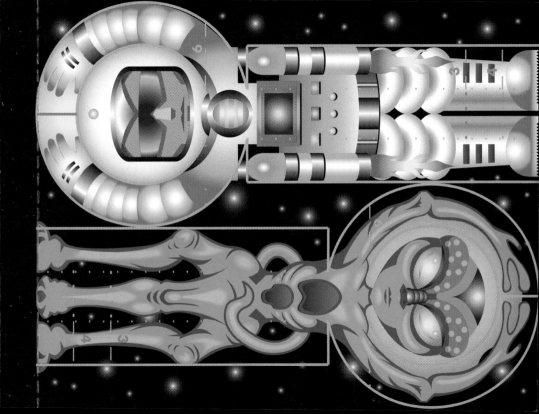

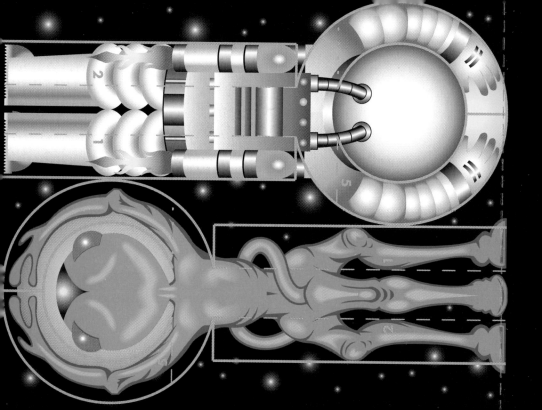

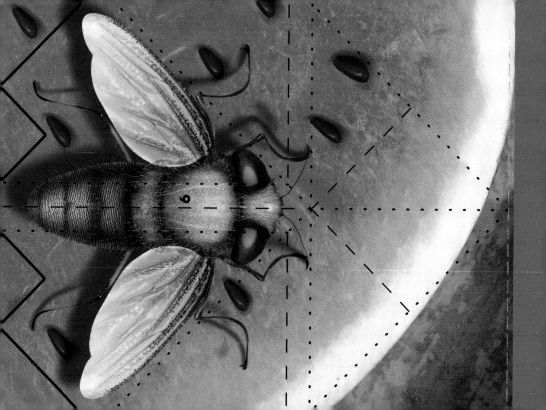

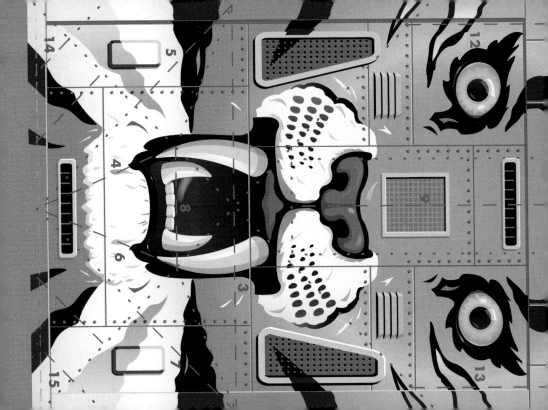

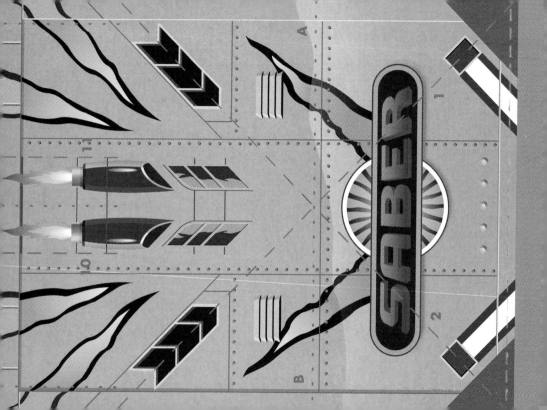

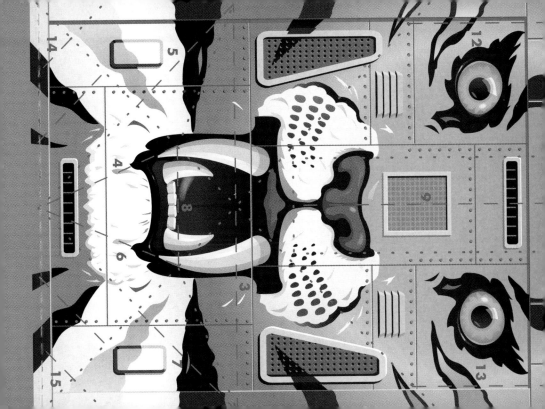

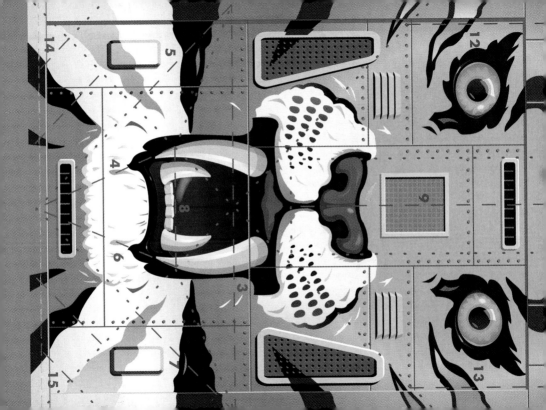

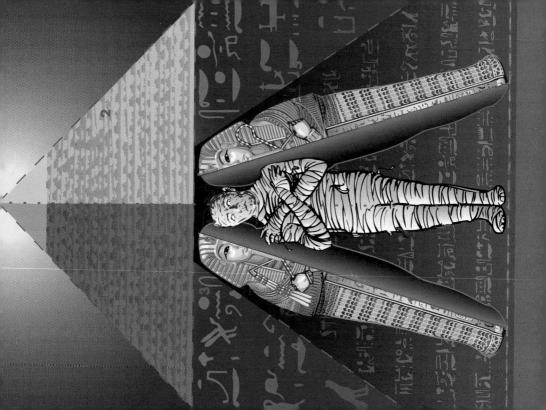

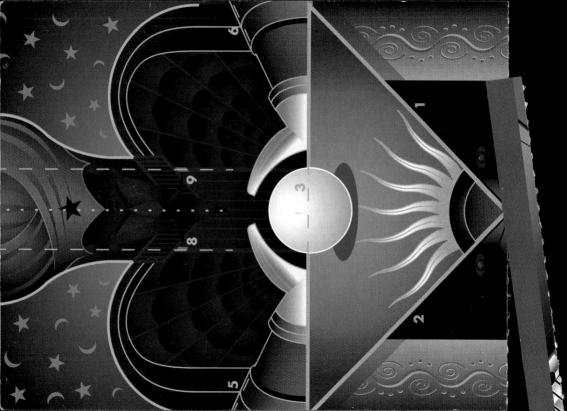

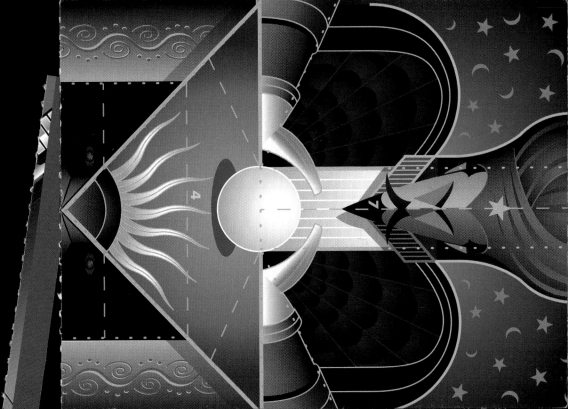

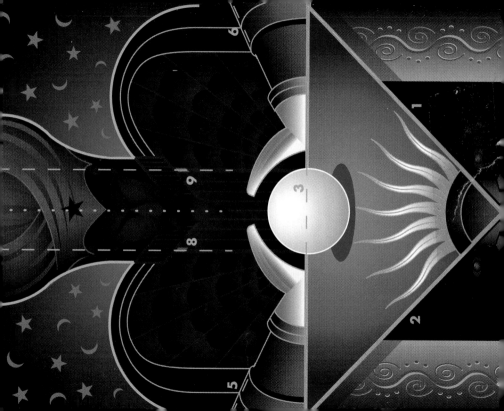

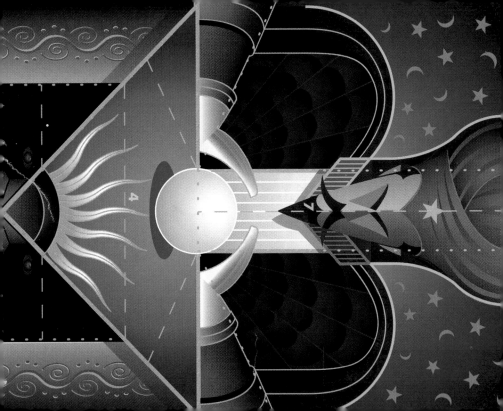

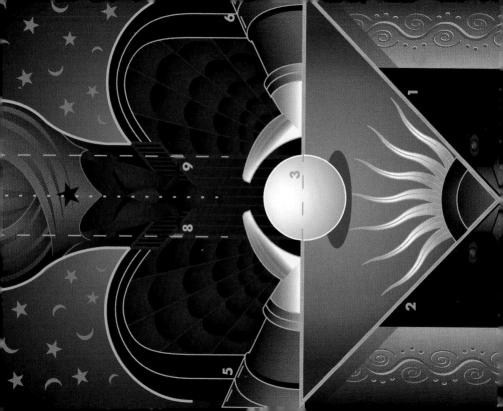

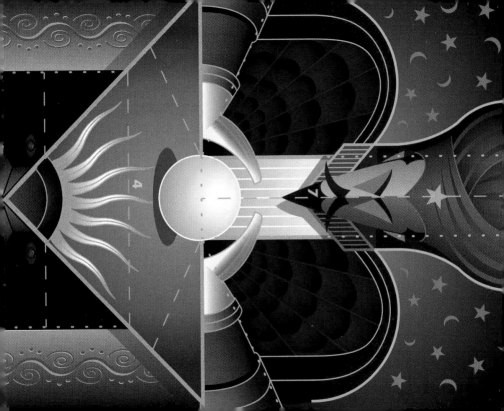

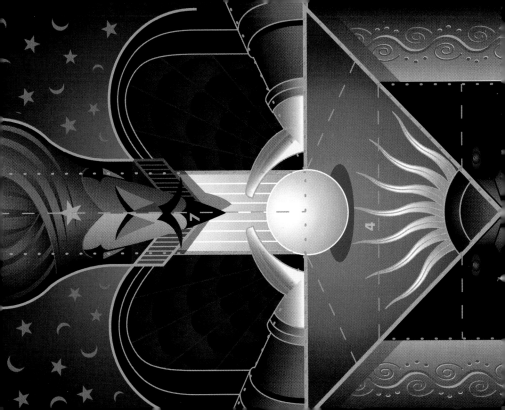

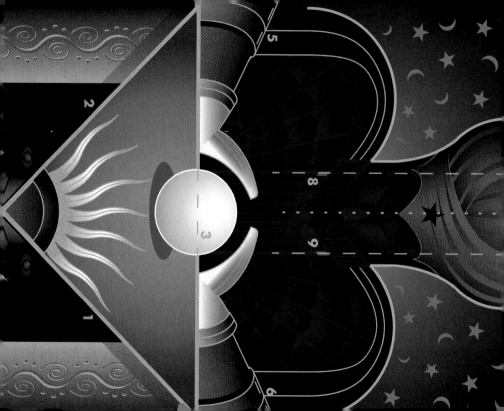

Phoenix

Phoenix

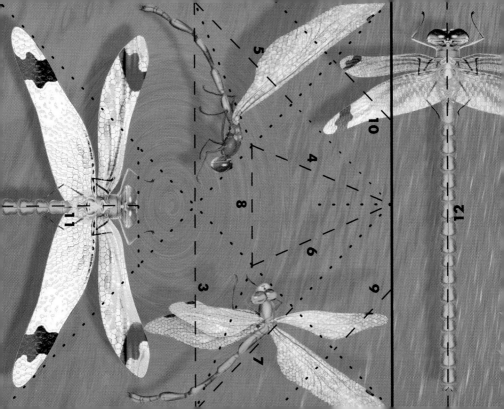

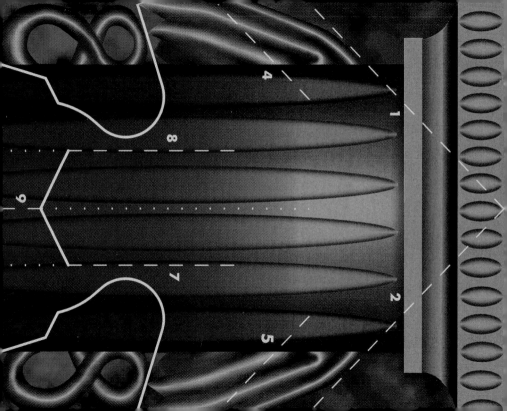

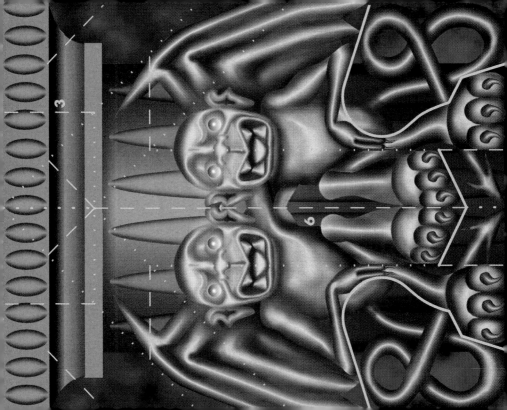

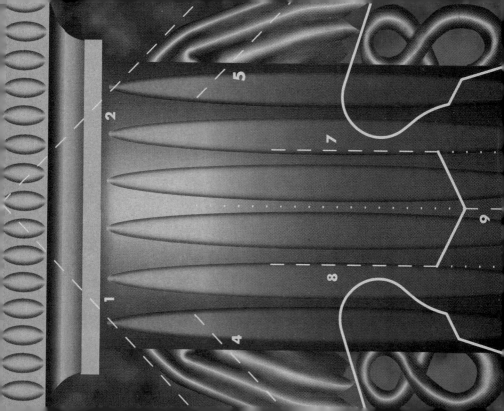

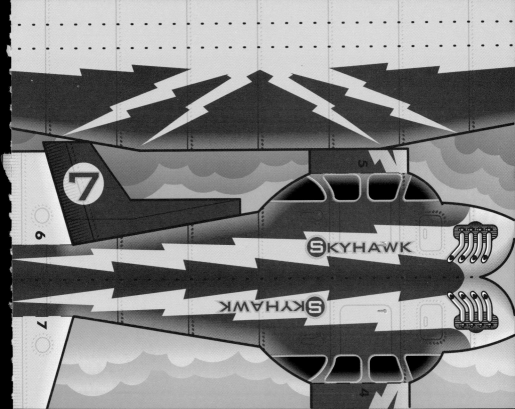

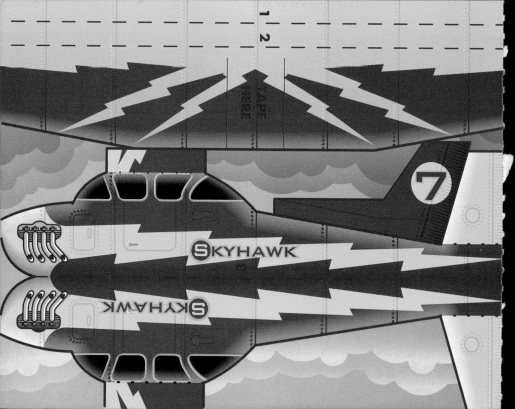

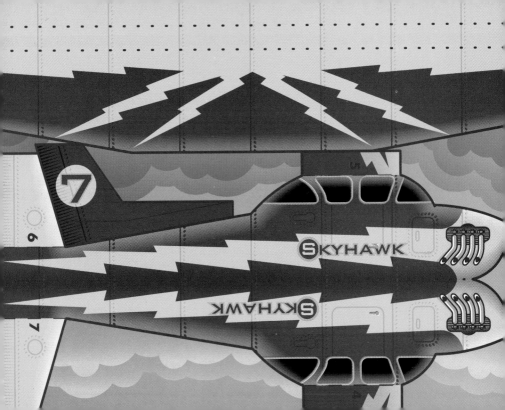

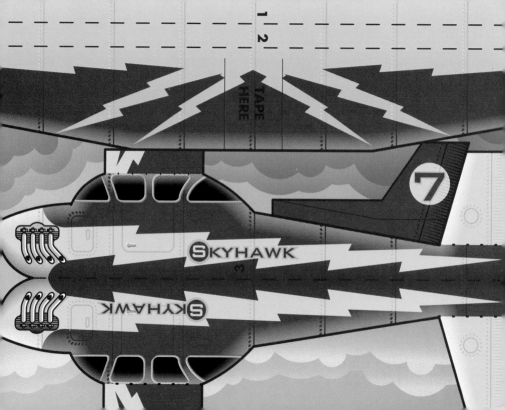

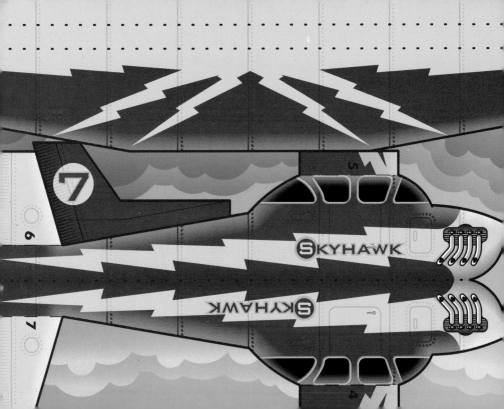

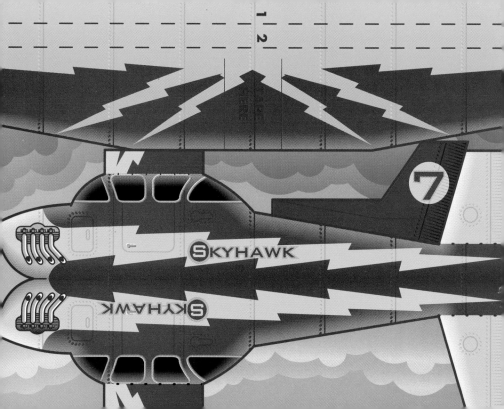

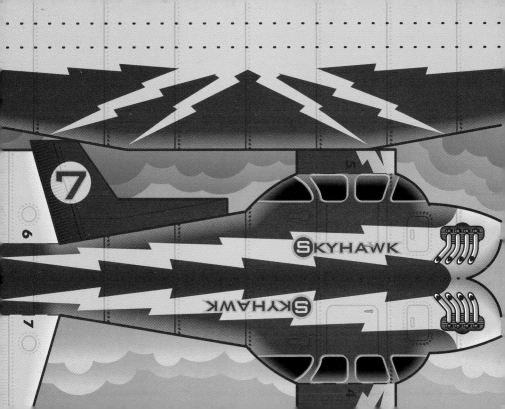

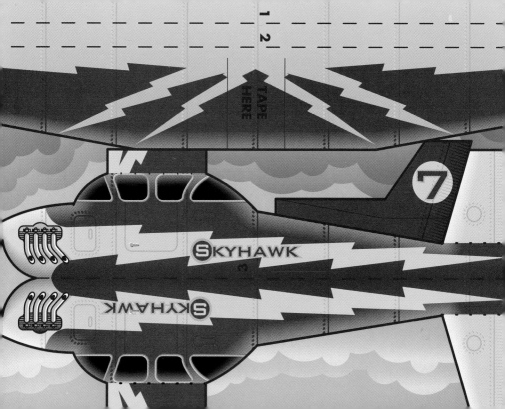

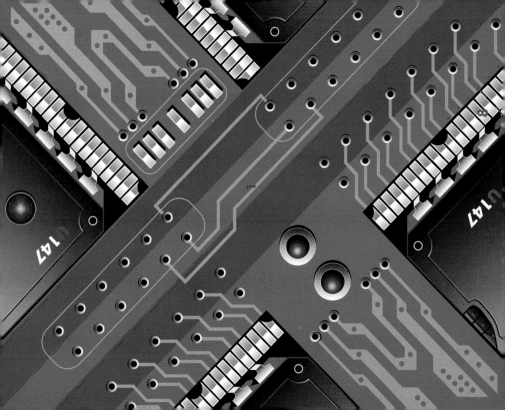

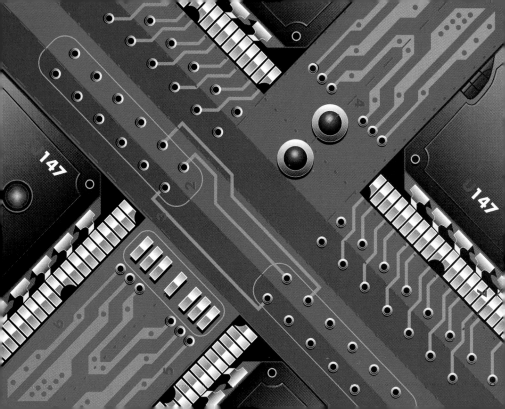

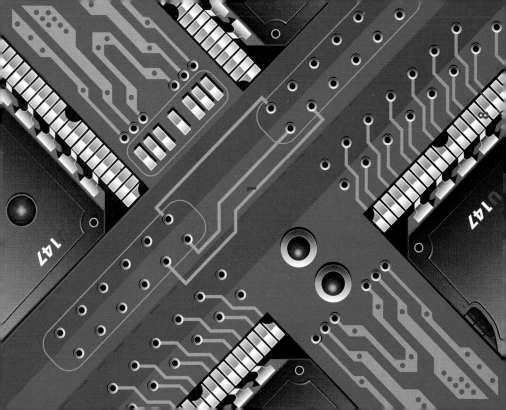

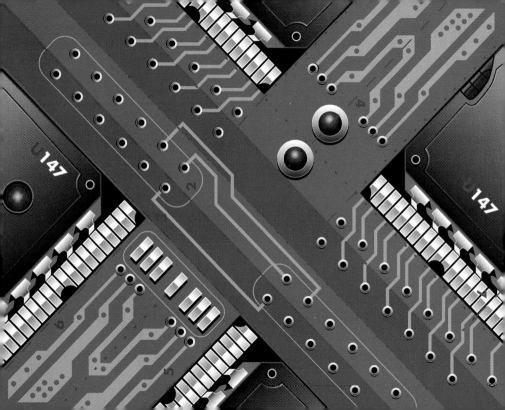

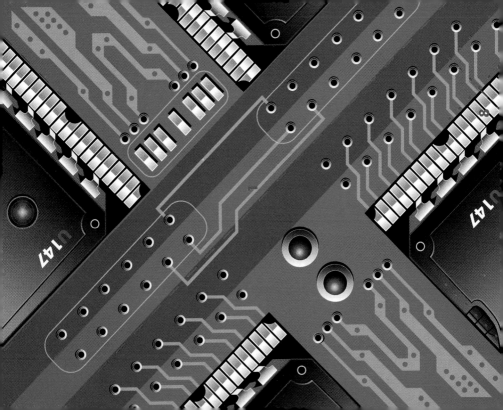

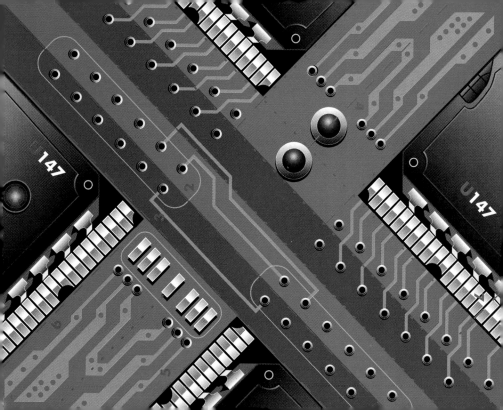